KARI DUMOUCHEL PARKER

God Reigns

Grace and Mercy
727-543-9860
kari.dumouchel@gmail.com

Table of Contents

Chapter One

Called to Holiness

How interesting a creature is man? Lord, You created a creature that is so magnificent. We have come from caves to the moon, from herbs to pharmaceuticals, pioneered medicine, science and literature. You value us. You desire an intimate relationship with us, with clay, with dust. It's Your breath that is in us. With tender, intimate love You leaned down and Your hands created and held our lifeless form. Your face touched ours as You exhaled life into our nostrils. The image of You leaning over Adam and that his existence started with intimacy shows me Your love for mankind and is very moving. You provided a planet that sustains us and meets all our needs. And Your design is that once death has claimed our earthly life, we will live eternally, with ageless bodies, with You. It's a hard concept that You could fashion us like a doll and yet imbue us with eternity, creating a creature so unique, with an inexhaustible capacity for enormous undertakings and accomplishments. We possess an unfathomable depth and complexity, because You, our Creator are unfathomable. We were made in Your image.

We are not like angels, yet angels were fascinated with us and broke heavenly laws to marry us and have their progeny, Nephilim.

I know that You are revealed in all of creation. This crazy, wild and wonderful planet called Earth that responds to man, his activity and even his sin. We are connected to this planet. It is our temporary home.

We are so important to You that when we chose a path that separated us from You, You sent us a Rescuer, a Redeemer. And not any redeemer, no, You sent Your Son. Why?

Life is about so much more than going to work every day. We are creatures of eternity, living out a speck of time that has purpose in our eternal design, here. Time and life on this planet are puny in the concept of all eternity yet our time spent here is hugely important to You. What could our purpose here be that is that important? Even when we say 'Yes' to You, there are deeper purposes. Time here is so fleeting, a speck of inconsequence when looked at from the vast scope of time and universes. A blink really. You want something from our time here. Is it because You want to spend eternity with a creature that, with all that we encounter here, all the temptations, the LIFE, that IN that life we CHOOSE You? Is that it?

Why all this? Sin, trouble and evil, why is this necessary? I don't understand Satan or evil, but I know that with evil, good is better understood and appreciated. Our souls long for goodness and justice. Life here can have heart-stopping tragedies for many. Not only are we a creature of unfathomable good and accomplishments, we are as equally capable of endless intrigue and unfathomable horror. This is a world full of danger, with vast chasms of evil, a world that harbors threats at every turn.

Yet, You tell us to live quiet lives, to work hard and to be at peace. Here?

To add to all this is that a relationship with You has no discernable path. This requires us to look for You, keep You center. Our paths are personal and individual for each of us. You have left us a guide, the Word and Your Holy Spirit, yet it requires our active participation. We must look for You, talk to You, knock on heaven's door and obey You.

I think our purpose here is to know You and to become holy.

A close relationship with You sculpts me so that I *become* holy. As a Father(another crazy concept for me), You know that a holy life brings my completion here.

"We are called into one hope, one Lord, one faith, one baptism, one God and Father of all." Ephesians 4-4

WHO IS GOD ~ HIS PERSONALITY

Below are some scriptures I found that help me have a glimpse of God:

"But the Lord is in His holy temple. Let all the earth keep silence before Him." Habakkuk 2:20.

"Bless the Lord, O my soul!
Oh Lord my God, You are very great:
You are clothed with honor and majesty,
Who cover Yourself with light as with a garment,
Who stretch out the heavens like a curtain.
He lays the beams of His upper chambers in the waters,
Who makes clouds His chariot,
Who walks on the wings of the wind." Psalm 104:1-3

Nature, weather and the sky always remind me of Him.

Did you know that God loves Israel so much that He has a pet name for Israel, Jeshurum (uprightness).

The Bible endlessly teaches me something new. I've read it cover to cover many times. Deuteronomy chapter 33 is an exciting narrative.

"The Lord comes from Sinai

And dawned on them from Seir

And shown forth from Mt Paran

He came with 10,000 saints

From His right hand

Came a fiery law for them

Paraphrasing, the chapter also says:

Jacob is the *place* of My inheritance.

God found him in a desert land, wasteland, a howling wilderness.

God kept him 'as the apple of His eye', hovered, spread His wings over him and carried him on His wings!

God is a poet and the Bible is full of love sonnets. The chapter goes on to speak of God lamenting when Israel left Him, their Rock and Creator and worshiped demons and new gods. God was heartbroken. It points a finger at me, and how easily I am led astray and let the world crowd out my love for Him, from His being my center.

I firmly believe that if the believer really understood God it would ignite their spiritual life.

Glory is often a description used for God. One definition of glory is magnificent splendor. There have been moments when I have been privileged to glimpse and experience glory. It's tied to moments where I have sensed and experienced God. It's overwhelming and ecstatic and rapturous. It's a difficult experience to describe because words cannot fully articulate it, it is so much larger than words. There's an energy that I feel as though it is pulsating out of my core, and it fills all my senses. I feel like I *must* be glowing. This is accompanied by tremendous joy and love. I don't get these moments often, but they are unforgettable and have punctuated my spiritual life. Can we all experience this glory? I don't know.

I had a spiritual renewal in 2006 and it sent me back to the Bible. It created this hunger to know God intimately, so I started rereading the Bible, from the beginning, looking for God. I wanted dimensions, definitions, a clearer image of Him, I wanted to *know* and understand Him, I wanted Him close.

Here is what I found:

- In Genesis I found El Shaddai, 'I AM Almighty God' which I understand the meaning of this is similar to the word for mountain; God's strength and endurance.

- In Exodus I found 'I AM Who I AM', the Eternal One, uncaused, independent, Creator of all things.

- He is 'The Lord', Jehovah, Yaveh, I AM God, merciful and righteous. Here He is revealing more of His character to Israel as their relationship grows.

- He is Adonai, Lord, Master with unlimited power and authority.

- He is Jehovah Jirah, our provider.

- He is Elohim, Exalted God. He is the Most High. 'I AM The Lord your God'. He is the Lord Who sanctifies, Whose name is jealous.

Israel did not call God by His name. They did not call Him Yaveh. Because of His holiness, they did not speak His name, they called Him 'Ja'. As in Hallelu *Ja.*

Here are some of the attributes I found:

He is merciful & gracious, longsuffering and abounding in goodness and truth, keeping mercy for thousands, forgiving iniquity and transgressions. The Lord will fight for you. The Lord is a warrior. He is a Husband. God is emotional. Read Exodus 32-33. He is called the God of the whole earth. He has created thousands of Universes, named the stars without number, planets are aligned perfectly to provide oxygen to our planet, the earth tilts and rotates to provide light and dark and seasons, and we are fearfully and wonderfully made.

CREATION

Genesis starts the creation story in its opening narrative.

"In the beginning God created the heavens and the earth. The earth was without form, and void, and darkness was on the face of the deep. And the spirit of God was hovering over the face of the waters." Genesis 1:1-2

Genesis unfolds the story that in six days God creates the Earth. It's first told how He caused light to enter this darkness and He then separated the light from the darkness. He created a firmament in the midst of the waters and separated the waters under the firmament and above. The firmament above He called heaven. Next, He gathered the waters together so that dry land would appear. The dry land God called Earth. The gathering of the waters He called seas. He then called for the land to bring forth grass that yields seeds, and fruit bearing trees. God then created lights in the firmament (heaven) to divide day from night and for signs and seasons, days and years. God next filled the seas with living creatures and the sky with birds. The following day God filled the land with land creatures. God blessed them and told them to be fruitful and multiply.

Lastly, God said "Let Us (God, Jesus and the Holy Spirit)make man in Our image, according to Our likeness, let them have dominion over the fish of the sea, over the birds of the air, and over all the cattle, over all the earth and over every creeping thing that creeps on the earth." Genesis 1:26

There is a mystery to the Creation story but when we begin to know God, we believe Him.

One of my personal favorites that talks about creation is the last 3 chapters of Job, which always thrill me. In these chapters God is talking to Job and his companions. It starts in chapter 38, in verse 2:

God says "Who is this who darkens counsel by words without knowledge? Now prepare yourself like a man; I will question you, and you shall answer Me. Where were you when I laid the foundations of the earth? Tell Me, if you have understanding. Who determined its measurements? Surely you know! Or who stretched the line upon it? To what were its foundations fastened? Or who laid its cornerstone, when the morning stars sang together, and all the sons of God shouted for joy? Or who shut up the seas with doors, when it burst forth and issued from the womb; When I made the clouds its garment, and thick darkness its swaddling band; When I fixed My limit for it, and set bars and doors; When I said, this far you may come, but no farther, and here your proud waves must stop! Have you commanded the morning since your days began, and caused the dawn to know it place, that it might take hold of the ends of the earth, and the wicked shall be shaken out of it?"

God continues in verse 16 "Have you entered the springs of the sea? Or have you walked in search of the depths? Have the gates of death been revealed to you? Or have you seen the doors of the shadow of death? Have you comprehended the breadth of the earth? Tell Me, if you know all this. Where is the way to the dwelling of light? And darkness, where is its place? That you may take it to its territory, that you may know the paths to its home? Do you know it, because you were born then, or because the number of your days is great? Have you entered the treasury of snow; or have you seen the treasury of hail, which I have reserved for the time of trouble, for the day of battle and war? By what way is light diffused, or the east wind scattered over the earth? Who has divided a channel for the overflowing water, or a path for the thunderbolt,"

Then in verse 28 "Has the rain a father? Or who has begotten the drops of dew? From whose womb comes the ice? And the frost of heaven, who gives it birth? The waters harden like stone, and the surface of the deep is frozen. Can you bind the cluster of the Pleiades, or loose the belt of Orion? Can you bring out Mazzaroth in its season? Or can you guide the Great Bear with its cubs? Do you know the ordinances of the heavens? Can you set their dominion over the earth?" In verse 36 "Who has put wisdom in the mind or who has given understanding to the heart?"

In stirring poetic language, God helps me look behind the curtain of Creation. It deepens my image of God, of His spectacular power, His knowledge and wisdom. He is still beyond my full understanding and comprehension. We are endowed with a finite mind. These scriptures are remarkable. I did not know that there was a treasury for snow or hail, that God set boundaries for the seas or that the morning stars sing.

Here, God is speaking face to face with Job!

It is an inspiring read and a beautiful narrative. I find myself in total awe when attempting to grasp all that God describes in these chapters.

Consider the created world, the world in our oceans with its bizarre life forms that undersea exploration is now discovering. When light enters this world, the creatures it illuminates are spectacular in their array of color and description! The huge jellyfish knock me out with their color, transparency, delicacy and grace. And it occurs to me, other than God (until now) who sees it? Color, flashing neon lights and fantastic beauty in the **dark**! But it must please God. I see a side of God that shows me His humor and His delight in His creation! I can see Him smiling and laughing. Until recently only God saw them.

Creatures that fly, buzz and hum, their vast numbers and they were *all* given natures and instincts. Everywhere I look I see the care and interest God put in everything!

Photographs of the universes that surround this planet, the galaxies, solar systems, black holes, supernovas, the vastness and beauty, the timeless quiet, stars and suns. How can anything but a living God explain this?

Our Father fills the earth, skies and the heavens with a glimpse (and it is just a glimpse) of His power, intelligence, beauty and majesty.

Nature has a voice and speaks His name and reveals to us God.

The gentle breeze that carries coolness, gently scattering petals, seeds and scents; moving and rustling like fingers through trees and tinkling with the sounds of gentle whispering chimes. It shows me the soft side of God. There are colors and scents that sweep in and peak out after the sleep of winter, ushering in spring. Flowers blooming with a riot of colors and aromas, trees clothing themselves with leaves, things greening up with new freshness. Then comes the warming of the sun as it moves closer to earth bringing with it long, lazy summer days. Even winter with its shortened days and long, cold nights brings a solemnity and mystery of the death of things, their deep sleep, its coldness and hushed closeness, clean and stark. We are reminded of beauty and purity when we look at the landscape of undisturbed newly fallen snow and the glistening icicles that drape and cascade acting as prisms reflecting color. There is a quiet reverence to the landscape. Winters and summers can offer us a time for reflection and contemplation.

The direct contrast to this is the fury and rage of weather, storms, hurricanes, tsunamis and earthquakes, their power and seeming unfeeling and impersonal wrath bringing destruction to all that lies in their path. With these comes an acknowledgement of our helplessness and puniness.

I think we understand that the earth is a living entity, but do we realize that the earth is connected to us and to God and is alive in a way we may not have considered? The earth responds to man for both good and bad. Does our sin bring about natural disasters?

"Let the heavens rejoice, and let the earth be glad;
And let them say among the nations, "The Lord reigns."
Let the sea roar, and all its fullness;
Let the field rejoice, and all that is in it.
Then the trees of the woods shall rejoice before the Lord,
For He is coming to judge the earth." 1 Chronicles 16:31-33

"For the Lord is great and greatly to be praised;
He is also to be feared above all gods.
For all the gods of the people *are* idols,
But the Lord made the heavens." 1 Chronicles 16:25-26

"Then, as He (Jesus) was now drawing near the descent of the Mount of Olives, the whole multitude of the disciples began to rejoice and praise God with a loud voice for all the mighty works they had seen, saying:

"Blessed is the King who comes in the name of the Lord!
Peace in heaven and glory in the highest!"

And some of the Pharisees called to Him from the crowd, "Teacher, rebuke your disciples." But He answered and said to them,

"I tell you that if these should keep silent, the stones would immediately cry out." Luke 19:37-40

"For we know that the whole creation groans and labors with birth pangs until now." Romans 8:22

"The heavens declare the glory of God; And the firmament shows His handiwork. Day unto day utters speech, And night unto night reveals knowledge. There is no speech nor language(peoples) *Where* their voice is not heard. Their line (sound) has gone out through all the earth, And their words to the end of the world." Psalm 19:1-3.

Yet there are those that deny Him? They choose the scientifically disputed theory of evolution. That we emanate from monkeys or slithered out of a pond.

Since my rebirth, I have become an avid camper and backpacker. I love being deep in the forest surrounded by the musty quiet. The occasional song of a bird aloft in a treetop causing me to look up and see the filtering sunlight through the trees, revealing the many shades of green as the light is defused in its descent towards the earth. I love climbing trails up mountains, following the switchbacks as they take me to the top where the trees open and offer breathtaking, panoramic vistas of the forest where I am greeted by cool breezes and stand shoulder to shoulder with the large birds of prey as they float and fly on unseen wind currents. I experience joy and happiness in these moments. I feel a strong connection to God and it has a sweet joyful, humbling quality to it.

Chesterton in Orthodoxy notes that God is ageless, and perhaps more like a child in His tireless delight in making thousands of identical daisies! God's spectacular way of opening and closing our days with those amazing sunrises and sunsets, and that no two are ever alike but they are repeated every single day. He paints this world to reveal Himself to us and to inspire us.

His wisdom is revealed in the order that is in nature and the timing of the seasons, the creation of all lifeforms, weather patterns; the countless species of insects and all forms and varieties of animal life, that each possesses natures and instincts, and their interaction with the cycle of life. Consider the variety of plants and trees that cover this planet. There are majestic mountains, deep valleys, shorelines, deserts and forests that are all teeming with life! Diverse beauty everywhere!

His greatest creation, us, with our amazing bodies and its capacity for emotion, thought, expression and imagination; the ability to create, to build, to subdue our surroundings, we see colors, we smell, all our senses, music and movement and mobility.

All of this makes our world interesting. Heaven must be awesome!

"All things were made through Him, and without Him nothing was made that was made." John 1:3.

ITS PERSONAL

And He wants a relationship with us. How to comprehend that?

Check out the Psalms because they are full of the attributes of God.

I try to spend time contemplating God. When I pray to Him, I try to imagine His face. I wonder about the color of His eyes. Is His face full of emotion or deep and fathomless? Does He have a countenance like a tempest and yet I know that it must be a face full of love and tenderness. Does He have a language? He sings, does He hum? And He made dogs!

"In that day sing to her
A vineyard of red wine
I, the Lord, keep it
I water it every moment
Lest any should hurt it
I keep it night and day" Isaiah 27:23

"For I know the thoughts that I think toward you, says the Lord, thoughts of peace and not of evil, to give you a future and a hope." Jeremiah 29: 11.

"The Lord your God us with you
He is mighty to save
He will take great delight in you
He will quiet you with His love
He will rejoice over you with singing." Zephaniah 3:17

He loves and cares for us so much.

"It shall come to pass
That before you call, I will answer
And while you are still speaking,
I will hear." Isaiah 65:24

There are times when I think about Who I am praying to, that I have *complete access* to Him? It shames me that I can be cavalier about that? When I go through very troubling times I sometimes imagine myself sitting on His lap, or resting against His chest, or hugging Him for comfort, or hiding under the shadow of His wings. Psalm 91. He is my Father and I'm His daughter. We are family. When I pray I also try to imagine the majestic and awesome throne of God, the glory emanating from Him as He sits on His throne and the magnificent heavenly beings that surround the throne worshiping Him, and God sitting listening to ME. How does this not knock us out! I feel His penetrating gaze, searching my heart, which causes honest communication. He knows everything about me. That's humbling.

This is the same God that talked and walked with Abraham, Moses and David. When I am dust, He will *always* be the same.

Amos 1:2 says "The Lord roared from Zion." This makes me smile, His emotion, His passion.

Amos 2:13 says "Behold I am weighed down by you, as a cart full of sheaves is weighed down." I can weary God with my sin!

Oswald Chambers says "God does not tell us what He is doing, He reveals to you Who He is."

"The Lord listened and heard them." Malachi 3:16. I love this scripture because I understand this to mean that when we talk about God to each other, His attention is focused on us and He leans down from Heaven to hear! Wow!

"But we all, with unveiled face, beholding as in a mirror the glory of the Lord, are being transformed into the same image, from glory to glory, just as by the Spirit of the Lord." 2 Corinthians 3:18. AMEN!

Oswald Chambers says, "God has ventured all in Jesus Christ to save us, now He wants us to venture all in abandoned confidence in Him."

"And His soul could no longer endure the misery of Israel." Judges 10:16. This scripture tells me that God suffers with our troubles and moves on our behalf.

Our relationship with God should be assertive and personal. God promises that if I will seek Him, He *will* be found by me. He promises to live in me and to be a constant companion. Like the song "I Can Only Imagine" says, the presence of the Lord is so awesome that it could make us dance, stand and sing, or His presence could make us stand still, be silent or fall on our knees.

Worship Him! Let the knowledge of Him fill you. Open your soul to let the Holy Spirit that resides in you reach heavenward to touch Almighty God. Give God room inside you. Give God time. Nothing in the world will any longer have any claim on you. Remember, we are just sojourners here. This is not our home. We are being prepared for glory and our heavenly home.

IMAGE OF GOD

I believe God is androgynous. Man was created in the image and glory of God. Woman was created in the glory of man.

How could God have sculpted the heart of a woman, nurturing, intuitive with such a capacity for love and mercy, gentleness, selflessness and tenderness, if those qualities did not emanate from Him? And tears, they don't just wash our eyes, they cleanse our hearts and souls, communicate sadness, grief, joy, laughter, frustration and even anger; all made and given by God Himself. There is the female form which is full of grace, beauty and softness, able to nurture and yet able to bear tremendous burdens. Our ability for communication, to delve into heart matters, soothe hurts and our intuition helps us to explain emotions to our male counterparts. We are the glue that holds together the world of our male counterparts. We are the heart and home's center.

And the male; they are the embodiment of strength, courage and leadership. There is stature in the male and he is endowed with instinctive qualities that provide shelter and protection, enduring great hardship and shouldering tremendous responsibilities. There is greatness in the male that is frontier. He is adventurous, leading in exploration, in discoveries and has moved this world forward in science, aerospace, medicine, industry, music and literature. Everywhere we look the world is stamped with the male enterprise, with his greatness. And other than God, only the woman can have mastery over his strong heart. God created this need in both to be completed by the other. The intimacy that can only be achieved in this relationship is the template for our intimacy with God. When we love each other selflessly and intimately, we come to understand something of the love of God.

"In the day that God created man, He made him in the likeness of God. He created them male and female, and blessed them and called them mankind." Genesis 5:1.

"God said "Let Us make man in Our image, according to Our likeness." Genesis 1:26.

"For this reason, I bow my knees to the Father of our Lord Jesus Christ, from Whom the whole family in heaven and earth is named." Ephesians 3:14-15.

"For a man indeed ought not to cover *his* head, since he is the image and glory of God; but woman is the glory of man." 1 Corinthians 11:7.

"For You formed my inward parts; You covered me in my mother's womb. I will praise You, for I am fearfully and wonderfully made;" Psalm 139:13-14

We were created by God for God.

How can the creation be more exciting or interesting than its Creator?

"For the Lord your God is God of gods and Lord of lords, the Great God, mighty and awesome." Deut. 10:17!!

RELATIONSHIP

Genesis notes that, after creating Adam, God would look for Adam in the Garden of Eden, to walk and talk with him! God looked forward to his companionship. He loved him and His love for man has not diminished. This sends a warmth through me.

A relationship with God is very similar to romance and marriage on earth. The 'Song of Solomon' is the only romance book in the Bible. God created romance and sex so that a man and woman could unite intimately and become one. When we are saved we enter an initial 'First Love' stage, full of heady highs, warmth and excitement for our beloved. As time progresses the bloom of the initial 'First Love' starts to pale both in our spiritual walk just as the pheromones dissipate in male/female relationships after a few years of marriage. We need God to deepen our marriage and create true intimacy, keeping alive the romance. It takes work, interest, dedication and commitment. The same is true with our relationship with God it takes work, interest, dedication and commitment.

"For your Maker is your husband, The Lord of Hosts is His name; And your Redeemer is the Holy One of Israel; He is called the God of the whole earth." Isaiah 54:5.

Madeleine and I have monthly fellowship where we meet for coffee and spiritual discussion. She was commenting this last evening about God, about His freshness, like clean flowing water. How healthy He is and how healthy we become in Him.

The throne room of heaven is described in Revelations 4:2-11: "and *One* sat on the throne. And He who sat there was like a jasper and a sardius stone in appearance; and there was a rainbow around the throne, in appearance like an emerald. Around the throne were twenty-four thrones, and on the thrones I saw twenty-four elders clothed in white robes; and they had crowns of gold on their heads. And from the throne proceeded lightnings, thundering, and voices. Seven lamps of fire were burning before the throne, which are the seven Spirits of God. Before the throne there was a sea of glass like crystal. And in the midst of the throne, and around the throne, were four living creatures full of eyes in front and in back. The first living creature was like a lion, the second living creature like a calf, the third living creature had a face like a man, and the fourth living creature was like a flying eagle. The four living creatures, each having six wings, were full of eyes around and within. And they do not rest day or night, saying:

"Holy, holy, holy,
Lord God Almighty,
Who was and is and is to come!"

Whenever the living creatures give glory and honor and thanks to Him who sits on the throne, who lives forever and ever, the twenty-four elders fall down before Him who sits on the throne and worship Him who lives forever and ever, and cast their crowns before the throne, saying:

"You are worthy, 0 Lord,
To receive glory, honor and power;
For You created all things,
And by Your will they exist and were created."

"And may you have power to understand as all people should, how wide, how long, how high and how deep His love really is. May you experience the love of Christ though it is so great you will never fully understand it. Then you will be filled with fullness of life and power that comes from God." Ephesians 3:11-19

It's our choice to follow God and to be obedient. His desire is to answer every single need and to be in every area of our lives. He made us and only He knows how to fix us. But we must take a step towards Him He is worthy to be worshiped and to have all of us.

Chapter Two

The Path to God

"Enter by the narrow gate: for wide is the gate and broad is the way that leads to destruction, and there are many who go in by it. Because narrow is the gate and difficult is the way which leads to life, and there are few who find it." Matthew 7:13-14

Our spiritual life is a journey.

I think the above scripture is generally accepted as a scripture related to salvation, but I also see this scripture in relationship to our spiritual journey.

Because I believe that life and our spiritual walk *is* a journey, I also believe that throughout this journey there are many obstacles, detours and derailments. These events are integral and intimately connected to the person God is sculpting. Just as exercise improves my physique and education improves my mind, difficult moments bring about my change. *That change is intended to bring me closer to my God.*

The path to holiness is hard because several things are happening. One is my personal sin which I must face honestly, examine what rules me, what I serve and what has control. This is always difficult and sometimes painful. Two, there is an enemy at work that will work diligently to keep my growth from happening.

Three, the world and all its enticements. World influences, the enemy and my personal sins are not easily recognized.

During difficult events our ability to receive holy revelation can be enhanced. God uses difficulties to get us alone with ourselves and alone with Him.

Difficult events are common to us and we all experience them. My son came down with Spinal Meningitis when he was twenty-two months old. When he was admitted to the hospital he was unconscious. They had to test different antibiotics and time was crucial because permanent brain damage and death occurred quickly with this illness. At the news of his condition, life took on a surreal haze for me. He had lapsed into a coma and the time line for his arousal from unconsciousness passed. My family lived on prayer and hope.

It was during this time that a friend put the book of Job into my hands. As I sat in the hospital room, I read the entire Biblical account of Job. It turned out to be a lifeline for me spiritually. In one day, Job had lost his ten children, his entire wealth and his standing in the community. That not being enough, his body was also afflicted with boils and his wife told him to 'curse God and die'. Hope gone? I think for most of us it might have been but not for Job.

The book of Job documents *conversation* between God and His creation(Job).

I was moved with Job's faith in God and awed by God's confrontation with Job. It ignited my heart, God revealing Himself to Job, letting him have a peek at His power, and a glimpse of the creation of earth. My mind started to grasp and understand that I had a powerful and mighty God. I felt the point of the book of Job was God communicating to Job, before He had restored anything to him, that He, **God**, was enough.

In-spite of Job's devastating losses, God was communicating to Job a more important message that *He alone was able to surround Job, interface with Job as only a Creator with His creation can.*

I knew then that God would be able to bring me through this crushing darkness. As incomprehensible as it is for a mother to lose a child, I knew in that hospital room that He would take care of me and that things would be okay. My son survived but through this experience I came to understand that if I had lost my son, my children, all I had, this God that was being revealed, was more than able to enter my heart and heal it and that the future possessed the hope of being made whole because *God would be enough.*

There are many difficult events we encounter throughout life. They can be our personal sins, failures, loss of family, hurts, friends or financial setbacks. But it is the *choices* that we make during and because of those events that make all the difference in their outcome.

While we may think we are here to have a career, find a mate, raise children and plan for retirement, we are here to develop a relationship with Jesus Christ and a by-product of that process is the refinement of our characters.

Careers, families and life are tools that He uses to chisel us into His children, to help us take on the family resemblance.

Life here is school for eternity.

Once we have accepted Christ as our Savior we are just at the starting gate on our spiritual journey. When we accept Jesus Christ as our personal Lord and Savior, a transaction has occurred, we have surrendered the lordship of ourselves to Him. With this surrender comes the *realization* that we are sinners and the *acknowledgement* that we need a Savior.

"Unless one is born again, he cannot see the Kingdom of God." John 3:3.

"He who finds his life will lose it, and he who loses his life for My sake will find it." Matt 10:39.

"Holy Father, keep through Your Name those whom You have given Me, that they may be one as We *are*." John 17: 11.

And also "that they all may be one, as You, Father *are* in Me, and I in You; that they also may be one in Us." John 17:21-23.

"..that they may be one, as You, Father, are in Me, and I in You, that they also may be one in Us." John 17:11. This is a prayer that Jesus prayed to His Father for us.

God says that oneness with the Trinity is possible. God will fulfill the prayer His Son prayed.

IT'S A PERSONAL JOURNEY

If we say yes to God, we have surrendered our lordship of ourselves and broken allegiance with the world. The Holy Spirit now resides in us.

But we can stop here in our spiritual journey, at the starting gate, never entering the race, let alone finishing. Or we may start out running, get discouraged or disillusioned and fall back into old worldly ways, fall asleep. Discipleship and a church family are crucial for growth.

Our journey reminds me of John Bunyon''5's book "Pilgrim's Progress". In his book he illustrates the Christian's journey towards Jordan (heaven) and the pitfalls and problems that are common to men and woman. There is an 'effort' that we must initiate in the same way that we arrive at any destination. As we travel on this journey, our spiritual lives will grow, deepen and strengthen. I believe that our spiritual life should mature and that it can be accompanied by moments of spiritual highness and holiness that is manifested by indescribable joy and inner peace.

As we mature our attachment to this world and sins can diminish.

Whatever we face on our journey, God is getting at something and it may frighten us. We may close and bar the door to this event, protecting some hidden desire, fear of loss, inordinate affection, a love or hate, even the desire to sustain some bitterness or un-forgiveness. When we allow God to show us what He is getting at and obey and follow Him in what is being revealed, we will find that whatever it is, He will heal or free us of the event or sin, and we have moved forward on our journey. God desires that we walk in freedom and liberty and oneness with Him.

"but as He who called you is holy, you also be holy in all your conduct, because it is written, "Be holy, for I am holy."" 1 Peter 1:15-16.

"let us lay aside every weight, and the sin which so easily ensnares us, and let us run with endurance the race that is set before us, looking unto Jesus, the author and finisher of our faith," Hebrews 12:1-2.

> "When I kept silent, my bones grew old,
> Through my groaning all the day long.
> For day and night Your hand was heavy upon me;
> My vitality was turned into the drought of summer.
> I acknowledged my sin to You,
> And my iniquity I have not hidden.
> I said, "I will confess my transgressions to the Lord.'
> And You forgave the iniquity of my sin.

For this cause everyone who is godly shall pray to You
In a time when You may be found.
Surely in a flood of great waters
You shall not come near him.
You are my hiding place.
You shall preserve me from trouble;
You shall surround me with songs of deliverance.
I will instruct you and teach you
In the way you should go;
I will guide you with my EYE." Psalm 32:3-8

When I had this epiphany in 2006 this scripture was given to me by a friend saying God had this message for me. Let me provide my interpretation of the above scripture:

When I hid my sin from Him, my body responded with illness
Because of Gods love for me He pursued me heavily
I finally acknowledged my sin & He forgave me
As a result, Gods covering protects me against all trouble
He delights over me AND He guides me with HIS EYE.

IT IS PERSONAL!

We were made for holiness and union with God.

BROKENNESS

I describe difficult events as breaking moments, simply put, brokenness. What is brokenness? As Christians, I believe that brokenness is events in a *process* that God uses to destroy sinful behavior, life strongholds, our imperfect beliefs and flawed personal truth with freedom and empowering us with His truth.

We usually have two choices when bad things occur. We can decide a negative approach that results in a negative outcome or we can decide that there is something of value occurring, a lesson to be learned, face it and allow what is happening to teach us and by teaching us, heal and set us free.

We need these breaking events because they free us from childhood events and flawed teachings that influence and ensnare us. It may be helpful to look at them this way, that all events and experiences have formed layers that cover our human form. Our parents, familial generational sin, childhood events, abuses and our cultures are each a layer. Some events and situations can introduce patterns of sin that may have formed a stronghold. We enter adulthood covered, hidden and weighed down by the stuff of our life. We function in life underneath these layers and some have become walled strongholds.

There may be a harmful event or abuse that has left a scabbed wound that has never healed. The wound is a layer. The way we were loved or not loved has left a layer. Many things from our childhood will reach out to control and influence us as adults. Throughout our lives these layers will manifest themselves in situations, events or relationships. There may be moments where a hurt has been triggered as though someone stuck a finger in an old wound. The response to this can be a sudden uncontrollable reaction and unfortunately many things from childhood are buried so deep that we cannot identify the source nor name the problem. At the eruption of a hurt, pain or anger it may leave us feeling out of control, unable to bridle our emotions or fears. It makes us victims.

Years ago, I remember the news reporting on a story about a runner who was kidnapped while running mountain roads. The young man, who had kidnapped the runner, it was learned, had intended to make her his bride. What was interesting about the situation was that the young man had grown up in a remote community that was not in touch with local or state laws. He grew up in a community that had managed to remain isolated and backward, deriving its laws, commerce and existence from its own internal society. I remember the commentary on the news at the time asking the question what law applied to this young man? His argument may be that that is how he grew up.

What we learn in childhood becomes our adult belief system, our personal law or personal truth that guides us.

These personal beliefs are the premise for how we see the world around us and assist us with the day-to-day running of our lives. These personal beliefs are expressed through an internal voice that helps us justify our thoughts and behavior. It influences our mind and emotions so deeply that we are not able to discern the truth or source of them. If we were harmed, we learned to be fearful and distrustful. If we were not loved or experienced ridicule in childhood, we may have developed self-esteem or rejection issues and now have trouble with relationships and boundaries.

The list and layers can be extensive and varied. This internal conversation formed in our subconscious becomes a conversation *to* ourselves that tells us a way to see or understand people, events and ourselves. This could be a belief that we have some superiority, or some unworthiness, that certain types of people are this or that, that to obtain love is tied to certain things or behavior. For some, the belief can be rooted in fear.

If we stop and listen to our thoughts, we will start to see a pattern in this internal conversation that feeds and influences us; a pattern of negative thinking, judging, superiority, low self-esteem, fearfulness, complaining and murmuring, faultfinding, etc. When events occur, our internal voice will communicate to us a way to understand what just happened or how to react to what just occurred based on what our *belief* is about the situation.

Very often our personal beliefs are not centered in truth.

Throughout life we receive information continually and they ramble around inside us to be *reconfigured* by our personal beliefs. It is not unusual for information to become distorted from what was originally received. Unfortunately, we think what we understand is true.

Often these 'layers' can cause us to run, medicate or turn to worldly experts to answer or cure our problems. It's like putting a band-aid on cancer. It may have a placebo benefit initially but it has no curative power.

PROBLEM AREAS

The areas that we want to protect and keep hidden can be many things. They can be a habit, an activity or an interest that we know if Jesus were visiting our home we wouldn't discuss or invite His review or reveal to Him. Some areas are fun, enjoyable and we may take solace or happiness from them. Some may be our obsessions, our entertainment or activities that keep us busy or occupied. Perhaps alcohol, sex, spending or finances are our areas.

He will reveal areas that are buried deep, some may have even seemed harmless. We may have engaged in some patterns of sinful behavior for so long that we no longer see it as sin. Some layers are areas that we love, that we have constructed to protect ourselves, places in our imagination where we hide and take comfort from the world; our refuge. These areas are not necessarily sin. They can be noble, but not God's, standards that we have erected even a 'persona' that we have created etched out by hurts and pains or by self-image issues, a 'persona' we hide behind but who is not the real person God intends us to be and often these can keep us trapped.

Whatever the area is, sin, our layers and personal truth are *barriers* to the working of the Holy Spirit. They're in conflict with the person God created us to be. They must go because, while some are not necessarily sin or evil, if they are not of God, they will stand in the way of God's will and purpose for us.

As God pulls close, the truths He communicates can become diverted by our 'stuff'. If His truth becomes influenced, obscured or colored by our personal beliefs, it will not remain His pure truth but will be tainted by ours. Our wrong beliefs will reconfigure His truth. We see this all the time in cults and disputes that separate Christians and often in politics; one believes one thing and another believes something else. There is one truth in God. As we grow in our relationship with God we will start to know *His* thoughts and *His* leading.

When God sent out the call for a servant, Isaiah heard the call, not because it was directed to him, it wasn't, he heard the call because he was listening and focused on God. When God asked for a servant Isaiah heard and said, "Here I am, Lord, send me." Can we get there?

As God destroys layers He is creating a humble person. In the destruction of our old nature, in not having an opinion of our self or a belief in our personal gifts and strengths, this allows God to be reflected in us unhindered by us. I find when I bring no agenda to the table in my interaction with people, not feeding anything in myself nor feeding anything with others, to please, control or manipulate, that there is a pureness and honestly that surrounds the encounter. God can use and speak through me unobstructed by me, my ego, fears, pride or personal opinions. *He wants an unobstructed voice to deliver His message.*

GOD IS OUR HEALER / OUR PSYCHIATRIST

The good news is that there is help and hope that we can be set free from these layers and strongholds. The cure to freedom and wholeness is Jesus Christ. As our Creator, He will heal our wounds, cleanse and restore us.

When we are saved our hearts and minds are transformed in the transaction, we take on the mind of Christ. You may start to notice that you can tell another Christian by their conversations, by their beliefs and by the way they see an event. It will line up with the same truth that lives in you. We are part of God's family. We recognize each other because we are related.

As we run our race God will orchestrate the process of removing sin, strongholds, de-layering and transforming our personal beliefs. The timing and completeness of this varies with each of us. We have a free will and we can refuse God's help. We can stand stiff-necked and two-fisted in the face of God or we can face the problem and let God have His way and set us free. Even though we are saved and His, we can still refuse and ignore God, consciously or unconsciously. We may stand as sentinel over the idols in our lives (and idols are anything that separates us from God, it is another master or love we serve). God will not make us do anything. He will not violate our will. He wants us to love Him and trust Him freely.

Trust, faith and obedience are *keys* to a higher spiritual life.

As we grow spiritually and lean into Him, we will find Him handling the day-to-day details of our lives. As we learn to trust Him our faith is deepened. We start to acquire a *history of victories, spiritual successes and answered prayer, which transforms our beliefs and* lays the *groundwork that convinces us we can trust God.*

God engineers the process in creative ways. I had trouble with a quick temper. I was led to a book about anger that taught that at the moment the temper flared I needed to understand the mechanism that triggered it. Once I discovered the source that jumpstarted the anger, identified the button, it stopped being a problem. Truth sets us free.

We shut the door to God when we protect a sin or a secret area in our life and this will prevent spiritual growth. Any area that we do not allow the penetrating gaze of God to illuminate will ensnare our steps and stop growth.

If we are honest with ourselves we realize that we welcome God in our home, into the living areas, but He is not allowed entrance to our secret closet or upstairs rooms. We happily show God our home but skirt Him past rooms, hurriedly close doors or sidestep hallways. To these areas we stand blocking Him. We are afraid of exposure and the loss of something that we think we care about or enjoy. We may even tell ourselves 'My lifestyle is better than my neighbor.' 'My sin is a small sin compared with so and so'. We may have developed a bell curve for the sin in our lives. But when we allow God in, His standard will reveal the truth to us.

If we allow the Holy Spirit to convict us in an area and we confess this sin, true contrition and repentance will cleanse us and this is the experience of brokenness.

"The sacrifices of God are a broken spirit, A broken and a contrite heart-These, O God, You will not despise." Psalm 51:17.

"My brethren, count it all joy when you fall into various trials, knowing that the testing of your faith produces patience. But let patience have *its* perfect work, that you may be perfect and complete, lacking nothing."
James 1:2-4.

Many of us are in the driver's seat of our lives, holding our lives together with glue and sheer will power. This 'something' being asked of us (letting go of the wheel) is the very thing we may have feared, and we see it as the complete dismantling of our lives and the world WE have created. We have worked hard to protect ourselves against life's failures, financial problems, relationship issues, health problems, emotionally and mentally, because our witness of the world indicates a determination to take us out. It is. The world is no friend to us. It belongs to the enemy. Our spiritual journey is teaching us we can trust in Him. The cleansing work of the Holy Spirit may also feel as though it has a destructive element. To some extent it does, it is dismantling our old selves and remaking us, new.

God does not need my help in running the universe. In fact I'm pretty sure He prefers it that way.

I am reminded of an image someone once told me that described a way to see the difficulties we experience. The image they gave was of an embroidered tapestry. While being made we can only see the underside with the stitching and cut and tied ends, but later, when it is completed and we view the finished product, we then understand the purpose for the difficult colors and tied ends, the breaks and changes in direction. We see that it all went together to create a beautiful work of art, a beautiful child of God and a reflection of our Father.

"He has delivered us from the power of darkness and conveyed *us* into the kingdom of the Son of His love, in whom we have redemption through His blood, the forgiveness of sins. He is the image of the invisible God, the firstborn over all creation. For by Him all things were created that are in heaven and that are on the earth, visible and invisible, whether thrones or dominions or principalities or powers. All things were created through and for Him. And He is before all things, and in Him all things consist. And He is the head of the body, the church, who is the beginning, the firstborn from the dead, that in all things He may have preeminence." Col 1:13-18

When the fullness of the above scripture becomes truth in us, we understand then that there is absolutely nothing more powerful that our Savior. Nothing. Nothing. Nothing. He is larger than any problem, pain, difficulty that we pass through. It stops our 'buts' and closes our mouths. He is above ALL things, more powerful than ALL things. Our journey is to Him.

The way to freedom and deliverance is no different than the way we refine gold through fire, or with the hammered stroke of a chisel create a perfect diamond, or through effort, discipline and education reach our chosen profession or become a winning athlete. There is a cost to achieving, obtaining, becoming. It is the same in our spiritual walk.

"My brethren, count it all joy when you fall into various trials, knowing that the testing of your faith produces patience. But let patience have its perfect work, that you may be perfect and complete lacking nothing."
James 1:2-4

$$\overline{}$$

Chapter Three

Barriers to Holiness

We struggle against Satan, our flesh and the world.

It is important to understand these and how they ensnare us.

Satan is the enemy of God Almighty and the enemy of man. He became god of this planet in the Garden. He is not omnipresent, he has an army of demons throughout the world to accomplish his goals. They are everywhere and in every segment of our lives. Most of us give him and them little thought. This, no doubt, is part of his plan. If he does not exist, then we will not be effective in combating his efforts and activities in our lives. We will not be able to understand those snares and strongholds in our lives that are his design, that have his stamp, his control. He is determined to either destroy us or to make us useless in the kingdom of God. The arsenal of the enemy is formidable and should not be ignored.

"Be sober, be vigilant; because your adversary the devil walks about like a roaring lion, seeking whom he may devour. Resist him, steadfast in the faith, knowing that the same sufferings are experienced by your brotherhood in the world." 1 Peter 5:8-9.

We have been born into the enemy territory. The religion of this land is busy trying to make us into their citizens, after their own kind, determined to remove our spiritual heritage and identity. Satan and his minions are relentless in their efforts to deceive and destroy us. They are at the heart of every vile, dark and evil deed. Satan was defeated at the Cross, but it is his plan to take as many of mankind as he can with him to his eternal dwelling place. Destination, hell.

Another area that produces struggles for us is our **flesh**. We are born into the heredity of sin lodged in our flesh. This is a result of the treachery in the Garden and is our legacy. It is what Paul wrote about in Romans 7:21-23

"I find then a law, that, when I would be good, evil is present with me. For I delight in the law of God after the inward man; But I see another law in my members, warring against the law of my mind, and bringing me into captivity to the law of sin which is in my members."

"For if ye live after the flesh, ye shall die; but if ye through the Spirit do mortify the deeds of the body, ye shall live. For as many as are led by the Spirit of God, they are the sons of God."!! Romans 8:13-14.

"To grant us that we, being delivered from the hand of our enemies, might serve Him without fear, in holiness and righteousness before Him all the days of our lives." Luke 1:74-75.

"For we know that the law is spiritual, but I am carnal, sold under sin. For what I am doing, I do not understand. For what I will to do, that I do not practice, but what I hate to do, that I do." Romans 7:14.

At the root of our flesh is pride which manifests itself in self-love, with co-conspirators ego and vanity. The roots of this self-love are like the roots of an old oak tree, intertwining and deep and it influences every aspect of our lives; it controls how we see ourselves, others and the world around us. We measure the world against ourselves, how things relate to us; and how others perceive us. We search for things, people and activities that make us feel happy; things that will titillate, stimulate and excite us. We are junkies to technology, TV, sports, celebrities and even politics.

Our world is surrounded at home, work and recreation with a focus on what makes us feel happy, safe, important. *It's all about us.* In our conversations we wonder how we are being perceived. "Am I liked, do they think am I smart or witty?" Our makeup, hairstyles and clothes occupy an inordinate amount of our time and thoughts. Where I live, what I drive, who my friends are, even how my children excel, are all a reflection of and all about ME.

We fear being ostracized, being outside the camp and not included and so we accept such worldly philosophy's as Evolution, Abortion, homosexuality and perhaps even the latest wave of anti-Christian sentiments (Merry Christmas as an example). We do not want to appear to be narrow-minded. We call this being politically correct; aligning ourselves with worldly doctrines to assuage our need to be perceived well and gain acceptance.

Pride, vanity and ego are at the heart of our human difficulties. I do not believe we were created to be this way.

I believe at the heart of this is looking honestly at ourselves and examining what motivates us, what influences us and what we are giving our allegiance to daily. It is unlikely that an idol will be dethroned if it is never identified. God says that the truth sets us free. It is the truth about ourselves in the light of The Truth, Jesus Christ, that will unlock our chains.

In our nightly prayers we ask God to forgive our sins but do we search our hearts to discover them? Then, do we honestly confess them? Do we want to be clean and set at liberty? Do we even know that we can be set free? If we desire to be clean and righteous freedom will happen.

It takes courage for me to look at myself honestly and to face issues that may lead to a breaking event. The Holy Spirit living inside me loves me and provides revelation. The Holy Spirit is that still, small voice.

The last area that wages war of with us is the **world** itself. Its influence on us is enormous. From our community, our society, our neighborhoods, churches, workplaces, television, schools, friends and relatives, all of these are influential in teaching us their beliefs. We are overwhelmed with information that forms alliances and doctrines in our lives. We belong to political parties, religious groups, clubs, organizations, affiliations, ideologies that line up with our personal beliefs.

Examples of worldly doctrines are Evolution, homosexuality and Abortion. They say something about me. Acceptance of these beliefs align me with the current, acceptable, politically correct crowd. Darwin's Evolution is a theory. Not a fact. Most of us have never challenged, investigated or actually read Darwin. The same is true of Abortion. Are we certain from information *personally* gathered, that the fetus is tissue at inception and not life? Evolution and Abortion are beliefs that have their core in our self-love.

"Where do wars and fights *come* from among you? Do *they* not *come* from your *desires for* pleasure that war in your members? You lust and do not have. You murder and covet and cannot obtain. You fight and war. Yet you do not have because you do not ask. You ask and do not receive, because you ask amiss, that you may spend *it* on your pleasures. Adulterers and adulteresses! Do you not know that friendship with the world is enmity with God? Whoever therefore wants to be a friend of the world makes himself an enemy of God. Or do you think that the Scripture says in vain, "The Spirit who dwells in us yearns jealously." James 4:6.

Our self-love is deeply rooted. We love us. Our self-love is the reason we protect ourselves. We measure ourselves against the world's standards. We are looking for happiness in things, events, people yet never truly satisfied because we are made in the image of God. Made *for* God. *Until we plug into God we cannot be truly fulfilled or satisfied.* In the same way that an appliance fulfills its purpose by being plugged in, we are not complete and fulfilled until we unite with God.

"Therefore, since Christ suffered for us in the flesh, arm yourselves also with the same mind, for he who has suffered in the flesh has ceased from sin that he no longer should live the rest of his time in the flesh for the lusts of men, but for the will of God." 1Peter 4:1-2

EVOLUTION

I believe that self-love is at the heart of the Evolution theory. This theory removes us from an accountability of being made in the image of God Almighty. If we were not made in God's image, if we slithered out of a pond or swung from a tree, it removes moral responsibility and spiritual parameters. If we are not made in God's image then we have no accountability to God, to find out about God, to search for Him and our purpose here.

Issues of morality, right and wrong are gone and this allows freedom to live life without moral boundaries. I am just an animal and when I die I am dust.

It gives license to explore our appetites. Right and wrong become a philosophical discussion and not a premise on which our social standards are grounded. Good and evil are just someone's perspective. We are lost.

"In the day that God created man, He made him in the likeness of God. He created them male and female, and blessed them and called them mankind." Genesis 5:1.

"God said "Let Us make man in Our image, according to Our likeness."
Genesis 1:26.

"For this reason I bow my knees to the Father of our Lord Jesus Christ, from Whom the whole family in heaven and earth is named." Ephesians 3: 14-15.

"For a man indeed ought not to cover *his* head, since he is the image and glory of God; but woman is the glory of man." 1Corinthians 11:7.

HOMOSEXUALITY

Another example of the worlds influence on our beliefs is the current social position that homosexuality is natural and that you are born that way. Scripture disputes this. God says that when we participate in these acts, we 'exchange the *natural use for what is against nature.*' God says that this sexual orientation is *unnatural.* I do believe that you can be born with the propensity for homosexuality the same as some are born with additive tendencies. To tell someone that they are born this way and is a natural lifestyle is to condemn them to a lifestyle without hope. If God says it is unnatural He has also made a way for deliverance from this lifestyle. Would we tell someone born with additive issues that it is okay to pursue that? As Christians we have a responsibility to the truth. We should offer a message of love and hope to those caught in this lifestyle and our message of hope lies in our alignment with God's truth.

"If a man lies with a male as he lies with a woman, both of them have committed an abomination. They shall surely be put to death."
Leviticus 21:13.

"Therefore God also gave them up to uncleanness, in the lusts of their hearts, to dishonor their bodies among themselves, who exchanged the truth of God for the lie, and worshiped and served the creature rather than the Creator, who is blessed forever. Amen. For this reason God gave them up to vile passions. For even their women exchanged the natural use for what is against nature. Likewise, also men, leaving the natural use of the woman, burned in their lust for one another, men with men committing what is shameful, and receiving in themselves the penalty of their error which is due." Romans 1:24-27.

Derek Prince notes in his book "War in Heaven" that Satan cannot harm God but he can harm *God's image* in us. He can get us to defile ourselves, addict ourselves and get us to rebel against God, this pleases Satan. He can get back at God through His creation, man. Evolution and other worldly doctrines are tools Satan uses to distance us from our God. He can then move freely amongst us to harm us because we are not anchored in truth and in the one who created us. Belief in these philosophies purposely gives us no pathway to God to reach out to for help.

ABORTION

The same is true of Abortion. There is no longer any question of abstinence and no moral boundary on our sexual conduct. I can remember a time when women pondered the morality of a sexual encounter. Now, more and more they are becoming the aggressor. And if a life is produced, it becomes a problem, an obstacle for the individual; an inconvenience and potential for the loss of freedom to the woman. Abortion activists cry it is a woman's right of choice. What they mean is her choice IS herself. Her *choices* were to abstain or use birth control, but once life is conceived, there is now another's right of 'choice' to consider. How is it that we are so blind to this fact? What woman, when she is having a desired child says "honey we are having tissue!" When it is desired it is a baby, when it is not, it is tissue.

There is such a dichotomy in this viewpoint on the innocent unborn, yet we are firm in our resolve to be blind about the conflicting messages. We adopt the worldly view of this because it serves our desire, which is our freedom to live life on our terms.

We tout this excuse that to abolish abortion is to step back into the dark ages of back-street abortions. I lived in the dark ages. I personally knew of very few women that had abortions then and it is unlikely that we would revert back to the back-alley abortions. Isn't it? We have really come too far for that. We have more information, medicine and support then was available at the time of our mothers.

But the pursuit of society in serving and satisfying self is the intent of the enemy of man. This doctrine of 'self-love' blinds us and promotes darkness and it is covering our Nation. Oddly history provides examples of civilization after civilization fallen to worldly doctrines and yet we still follow in their footsteps. Doomed for the same end. Satan has been around since mankind began.

But the scriptures dispute this determined attitude about the world's doctrines.

"For You formed my inward parts; You covered me in my mother's womb. I will praise You, for I am fearfully and wonderfully made;" Psalm 139:13-14

And verse 15-16 "My frame was not hidden from You, when I was made in secret, and skillfully wrought in the lowest parts of the earth. Your eyes saw my substance, being yet unformed. And in Your book they all were written, The days fashioned for me, When *as yet there were* none of them."

We existed before birth. There is no factual evidence otherwise, is there?

GOD CHIP / IMMORTALITY

The Word says that God has imprinted Himself in our hearts.

"He has made everything beautiful in its time. Also He has put eternity in their hearts." Ecclesiastes 3:11.

The immortality of God is planted in us and God has created the earth and heavens to reveal Himself. Who He *IS* is evident in the created world. There is an innate sense in **all** of us as to the truth of Evolution and Abortion *and God.* We cannot get to the truth of God through head knowledge but through the truth hidden in our hearts.

"..because what may be known of God is manifest in *them,* for He has shown it to *them.* For since the creation of the world His invisible *attributes* are clearly seen, being *understood* by the things that are made, *even* His eternal power and Godhead so that they are *without excuse* because, although they *knew* God, they did not glorify *Him* as God.." Romans 1:19-20.

"But you have an anointing from the Holy One, and you know all things. I have not written to you because you do not know the truth, but because you know it.." 1 John 2:20-21

"Today if you will hear His voice, Do not harden your hearts as in the rebellion." Hebrews 3:7-8.

"But I see another law in my members, *warring* against the law of my mind, and bringing me into captivity to the law of sin which is in my members."
Romans 7:23.

"The heavens declare the glory of God; And the firmament shows His handiwork. Day unto day utters speech, And night unto night reveals knowledge. There is no speech nor language *Where* their voice is not heard. Their line (sound) has gone out through all the earth, And their words to the end of the world." Psalm 19:1-3.

The above scripture tells us that Creation speaks to us! Creation speaks God's name! It says that there is no language (meaning people), who have not heard Gods voice; that it has gone out to all the earth and will till the end of the age. We will not stand before God and say we did not know Him nor hear Him calling. I believe more 'faith' is needed to believe in Evolution or Abortion than God Almighty; who is present and evident in all created things.

But there is a *cost* to living for God. We must face ourselves and the world and yield ourselves to God's kingdom. It is the breakdown of our old nature. We have a free will. We decide how far we go with God.

We are in a war.

We battle, first against the enemy, who is ever vigilant, secondly, against our flesh and thirdly against the world. The scriptures outline and reveal a life of victory, freedom and liberty where we live on a higher spiritual plane, walking and abiding daily, moment by moment in the Fruits of the Spirit; Gal 5:22

love, joy, peace, patience (longsuffering), kindness, goodness, faithfulness, gentleness and self-control.

If we seek God, He *will* lead our lives and fulfill all His promises. Every day we make decisions about a multitude of things. Every day we have to decide for God. We are to pray without ceasing (1 Thess 5:17*),* which is to literally talk to God all day! God wants us to put Him first in everything. As we start to run this race, we will come to find the prize of the higher calling of God in Christ Jesus.

PRAYER

I find when I have frank, honest, nothing held back conversations with God, that it always changes things, always. For the conversation to even occur, I have had to come to a place where I am willing to look at myself, be honest about my desire, be honest about the issue and lay it out before God. When we bring something out into the light it is never the same. And when we take the next step to talk about it with God, like confessing to a friend, we now realize we are accountable about the 'something'. We can no longer refute, ignore or pretend about it any longer. An example is AA, you must confess you are an alcoholic. The confession means you are no longer deluded about it. The conversation made it a reality. God knows what we need before we ask, but He desires that we still ask. It is 'in' the asking, in the communication, that we deepen about the matter. In the communication we are exposing ourselves and this 'something'. The exposure brings healing and accountability and the sharing is cathartic.

HOW TO IDENTIFY GOD

It is the work of the Holy Spirit to prompt the recognition of a sin or area to us. The Holy Spirit speaks to us in various ways such as a disturbance or conflict in us, disquiet or an internal checking in moving forward, a pause inside, a question. It is often something we sense unsettled, something nagging in the back of our mind, *something*. There may be a lack of freedom in making decisions, or having our conscience burdened about an issue.

Often with areas of sin we have heard a voice, felt a soft nudge and maybe more than once. This is the Holy Spirit illuminating possibly a sinful activity. He could be highlighting a need for correction or a closed door to future plans. It is not unusual to push the voice away or just ignored it altogether. In fact, our behavior may have silenced the voice for a season. But when the time comes when we turn back to God, eventually the penetrating voice of the Holy Spirit will re-visit the area and now we listen.

Develop a habit of listening so that the Holy Spirit's prompting and leading becomes a familiar voice to us. When God leads, the path has a certainty about it, there's cleanness, peace and confidence. If these are not present, pray for God's direction.

"I press toward the goal for the prize of the upward call of God in Christ Jesus." Philippians 3:14.

"When the enemy shall come in like a flood, the Spirit of the Lord shall lift up a standard against him." Isaiah 59:19.

Take hope! Everything we experience is common to man. Read Jeremiah 29:11-13. God has plans to deliver us, give us hope and a future. It is a promise. Jeremiah 29 goes on to say that we must call upon God and pray to Him, seek God and He will be found by us! God says He will listen to us. He says we will find Him when we seek Him with our whole heart. If we trust in God and put Him first He will lift us up, protect us from Satan and help us overcome our flesh. He has made a way for us to be free.

"Resist him (the devil), steadfast in the faith, knowing that the same sufferings are experienced by your brotherhood in the world." 1 Peter 5:9.

"But may the God of all grace, Who called us to His eternal glory by Christ Jesus, after you have suffered a while, perfect, establish, strengthen and settle *you*." 1 Peter 5:10.

"Therefore humble yourselves under the mighty hand of God, that He may exalt you in due time, casting *all* your care upon Him, for He cares for you."
1 Peter 5:6-7.

Chapter Four

Satan

I thought I would start this chapter with the numerous Biblical references to Satan. The Bible does not ignore him.

"How you are fallen from Heaven, O Lucifer, son of the morning!

How you are cut down to the ground, You who weakened the nations!
For you have said in your heart: I will ascend heaven, I will exalt my throne above the stars of God
I will also sit on the mount of the congregation on the farthest sides of the north;
I will ascend above the heights of the clouds, I will be like the Most
High!
Yet you shall be brought down to Sheol, to the lowest depths of the Pit."
Isaiah 14: 12-15.

"You *were* the seal of perfection, full of wisdom and perfect in beauty.

You were in Eden, the garden of God;

Every precious stone *was* your covering: The sardius, topaz and diamond,

Beryl, onyx and jasper, sapphire, turquoise, and emerald with gold.

The workmanship of your timbrels and pipes was prepared for you on the day you were created.

You *were* the anointed cherub who covers; I established you;

You were on the holy mountain of God; You walked back and forth in the midst of the fiery stones.

You *were* perfect in your ways from the day you were created, till iniquity was found in you.

By the abundance of your trading you became filled with violence within, and you sinned;

Therefore I cast you as a profane thing out of the mountain of God; And I destroyed you, O covering cherub, from the midst of the fiery stones.

Your heart was lifted up because of your beauty; you corrupted your wisdom for the sake of your splendor;

I cast you to the ground, I laid you before kings, that they might gaze at you.

You defiled the sanctuaries by the multitude of your iniquities, by the iniquity of your trading;

Therefore I brought fire from your midst; It devoured you, and I turned you to ashes upon the earth in the Sight of all who saw you.

All who knew you among the peoples are astonished at you; you have become a horror,

And *shall be* no more forever." Ezekiel 28:12b-19.

"For the accuser of our brethren, who accused them before our God day and night, has been cast down." Revelations 12:10.

"And war broke out in heaven: Michael and his angels fought with the dragon; and the dragon and his angels fought, but they did not prevail, nor was a place found for them in heaven any longer. So the great dragon was cast out, that serpent of old, called the Devil and Satan, who deceives the whole world; he was cast to the earth, and his angels were cast out with him." Revelations 12:7-9.

But Jesus says:

"I saw Satan fall like lightning from heaven. Behold, I give you the *authority* to trample on serpents and scorpions, and *over all the power of the enemy,* and *nothing* shall by any means hurt you. Nevertheless do not rejoice in this, that the *spirits are subject to you,* but *rather rejoice because your names are written in heaven."* Luke 10:19-20.

"*Assuredly,* I say to you, whatever you bind on earth will be bound in heaven, and whatever you loose on earth will be loosed in heaven." Matthew 18:18.

"For we do not wrestle against flesh and blood, but against principalities, against powers, against the rulers of the darkness of this age, against spiritual hosts of wickedness in the heavenly places." Ephesians 6:12.

"Put on the whole armor of God, that you may be able to stand against the wiles of the devil." Ephesians 6:11.

"Therefore take up the whole armor of God, that you may be able to withstand in the evil day, and having done all, to stand. Stand therefore, having girded your waist with truth, having put on the breastplate of righteousness, and having shod your feet with the preparation of the gospel of peace; above all, taking the shield of faith which you will be able to quench all the fiery darts of the wicked one. And take the helmet of salvation, and the sword of the Spirit, which is the word of God; praying always with all prayer and supplication in the Spirit." Ephesians 6:13-18.

"For though we walk in the flesh, we do not war according to the flesh. For the weapons of our warfare *are* not carnal but mighty in God for pulling down strongholds, casting down arguments and every high thing that exalts itself against the knowledge of God, bringing every thought into captivity to the obedience of Christ, and being ready to punish all disobedience when your obedience is fulfilled." 2 Corinthians 10:3-4.

"And these signs shall follow those who believe: In my name they will cast out demons; they will speak with new tongues; they will take up serpents; and if they drink anything deadly, it will by no means hurt them; they will lay hands on the sick, and they will recover." Mark 16:17.

"He called His twelve disciples together and gave them power and authority over all demons, and to cure diseases." Luke 9:1.

"Then the seventy returned with joy, saying "Lord, even the demons are subject to us in Your name." Luke 10:17.

"But thanks *be* to God, who gives us the victory through our Lord Jesus Christ." 1 Corinthians 15:57.

Be sober, be vigilant; because your adversary the devil walks about like a roaring lion, seeking whom he may devour. Resist him, steadfast in the faith." 1 Peter 5:8-9.

As the numerous above scriptures point out, Satan is real.

Lucifer (Satan) was one of the highest-ranking angels. He was an archangel of the stature of Michael. He was also beautiful. I understand that he may have been *the* most beautiful angel. However, his pride and vanity became so great that he determined to be God; to sit alongside the Most High even though he was a created spirit! He corrupted a third of the angels in heaven and started a rebellion. Some of these angels are now the demons that hound and trouble us. Satan is an angel of light and he can manifest himself to us in pleasing and unassuming ways. He tempts us and then feeds and fuels weak areas in our flesh. If we desire love, he will lead us to unacceptable mates or endless encounters that harm us. If our desire is peace, he may lead us into a false religion or cult that offers this. For every good and noble thing God has devised for us, the enemy has a cheap and dark duplicate. It is why he is not easily recognized. He is the master of deception.

The Holy Spirit in us will reveal areas under his control and influence and lead us to deliverance from them.

We should spend time reading these scriptures and asking for discernment of them. Daily I put the armor of God on myself and those I have spiritual guidance over.

DELIVERANCE

We have power and authority. Why? I believe because we are expected to use it.

I do not get the sense from reading scriptures that Satan does not exist nor that we are to do nothing with regards to him. In fact, the above scriptures seem to dispute this belief. Just as the disciples took authority over demons as part of their routine ministry, I believe that warfare is part of our spiritual lives.

I think it is impossible to live a full Christian life if we do not understand our enemy, the devil. Christ dealt with Satan routinely. He did not ignore him and nor should we. God has given us tools for warfare so that we can have victory over Satan.

There are a number of useful books available for the believer written by people to whom God has given this ministry. The fellowship of the brethren is full and diverse with each of us endowed with gifts that God uses in His kingdom here. I believe there are those God has given a ministry of spiritual warfare. I believe in spiritual warfare. I do not believe we should spend unbalanced time or attention here; but I do believe we should spend some time understanding, identifying and breaking demonic strongholds in our lives.

I suggest that you pray over God's will for you in understanding this subject. Find someone gifted in this area. I sat through deliverance early in my walk. Occasionally I take stock again of my lifestyle and check to see if I have given the enemy license in any area of my life. License would be whenever I have given consent to Satan in any area, become involved in sin where I have invited their presence in my life. Often, we do this unknowingly because Satan has been at this deception game a long time.

In the Garden, Adam turned dominion of this planet over to the enemy. We see the enemy's evil hand throughout history. Every evil, every horror, all the depravity of man from civilization to civilization, has its source in him.

Satan has set up a hierarchy of demons in stature from great to small.

In the book of Daniel chapter 10:12-14, speaks of a heavenly messenger(angel) who is delivering a message from God to Daniel. The messenger tells Daniel how a demon, the prince of the kingdom of Persia, had fought with him and the archangel, Michael, had to come and help him, enabling him to deliver this message from God to Daniel. The chapter goes onto report that the messenger will also fight with the demon prince of Greece.

I believe there are demons assigned to many things, including people, places, territories, objects and even countries.

I remember reading the 'Screwtape Letters' by C.S. Lewis which was a fun account of an older demon teaching his younger relation how to harass a young man to whom he was assigned. Daily the young demon would receive instruction or report the daily successes or failures of his assignment. I remember laughing when realizing that some of what the young demon was relating had just occurred to me that day. While this account was a fun read, Satan and his demons are not fun. They are vile and dark and full of horror. We should not consort with them in any way. We should walk in the light of our great Lord who has defeated Satan.

We are born with the heredity of sin in our flesh. But God has not left us alone. He has left us His Word and His Holy Spirit to deliver us and make us more than conquerors.

"For you did not receive the spirit of bondage again to fear, but you received the Spirit of adoption by whom we cry out, "Abba, Father.""

Romans 8:15.

My church helped me through deliverance years ago. We all have areas where we are oppressed by Satan and his minions. I had areas where I opened up to Satan in my youth culminating with drugs and mystical religions. I could feel pressure and a confinement of movement on my body. As part of my deliverance, I was asked to fast for three days and pray to discern strongholds. When the deliverance was over I felt joyful, free and weightless, as though pounds had been taken off my shoulders! I had also uncovered a personal core belief that was destructive. There were areas on my body where I felt a new freedom in movement as though something had physically held it confined and now my body had been released. Again, I believe it is important that you approach this with prayer and assistance.

Satan and his demons can gain a foothold in our lives in many ways. Certain sins have demonic attachments. I believe there are demons assigned to illicit drugs, improper sexual activity and even objects. There can be, as seen in Daniel, demons assigned to cities and countries. The fictional accounts of demons found in the Peretti books 'Piercing the Darkness' and 'This Present Darkness' I believe are interesting renderings of demonic activity in our lives. They are attached to certain emotions such as hate and rage, lust and greed. As our appetites in areas are fed by our continuing to participate in them, the demonic control can deepen and grow and move out into other areas and could eventually destroy us. The serial killer, Ted Bundy, says that his appetite for killing young women was born in pornography. As it was fed, it grew and developed new appetites that eventually controlled him and led him to murder.

Evil grows in darkness, in secret. But eventually it will have a desire to enlarge its scope and this is often how the secret lives and sins of people become exposed. Satan has no love for anything or anyone, no loyalties, there is nothing good in him. How could he possess any good or righteous qualities?

As I have said earlier, to get free we must take honest stock of ourselves, besetting sin, areas where we are easily tempted, areas where we struggle and let the Holy Spirit help to reveal strongholds and set us free. God already knows our areas so what is the point in keeping anything a secret? Why hold on to a trap or a chain the enemy is using to keep us from walking in liberty? Pray that God increase your understanding and give you discernment of all areas and then confess them and let God cleanse you and restore you.

Most deliverance is quite simple. But some may have involved themselves in darker areas where it is truly advisable to seek assistance from someone whom God has given this ministry. Once you have identified the demonic strongholds, simply confess them, and in the name of Jesus Christ break, shatter, destroy and cast off all demonic influences. It is only in the name of our Savior that we have any power or authority. Pray to have the influence broken and shattered completely, rebuking it and sending the spirit back to its home. I pray this as I do not want it free to roam my home or vicinity. I tell them to go to their home. Cleanse your house in the same way. Do not talk to them, other than to discern their identity, nor try in any way to communicate with them. There is no reason for this and it is unnecessary to break their hold on you.

You may find that some physical ailments will cease. I had pressure and a sense of heaviness on my body that I did not realize was there until it was removed. I do not believe demons can possess Christians, but I do believe that they can oppress them and their flesh.

Once you have prayed and received deliverance, pray protection from the Holy Spirit and guidance to help you discern the workings of the enemy and then leave the matter. I believe we can sense things dark, unclean and oppressive. When the Holy Spirit reveals them, rebuke and stand against them in the name of Jesus Christ.

Be mindful that the enemy is a resourceful liar. If he comes back to tell you that you did not get set free, rebuke him in the name of Jesus Christ. He may come back in some other area, but awareness and rebuke are sufficient. Remember, he is a defeated foe! But the Word instructs us to stay vigilant.

God has not given us more than we can endure. He has made a way of escape. Seek Him and He will reveal all as you pass through your trial or temptation. He will help you name the problem and show you the path to freedom and liberty. The truth sets us free. Often understanding a problem area in our life will end its control and influence.

I have a list of demons. I will note the list and leave it with the reader to seek additional help with this.

Spirit of heaviness -Isaiah 61:3
Spirit of jealousy - Numbers 5:30
Spirit of lying - 1 Kings 22:22
Perverse spirit - Isaiah 19-14
Familiar spirit - Lev 20:6, 20:27, Deut: 18:11, 1Samuel 28:3
Spirit of pride and haughtiness- Proverbs 16:18
Spirit of whoredom- Lev 19-29 & 20:5, Num 25:1; Hosea 1:2
Spirit of infirmity- Luke 13: 11
Deaf & dumb spirit- Mark 9:25 Spirit of fear- 2 Tim 1:7
Spirit of bondage- Romans 8:15
Antichrist spirit 1 John 4:3

We must be careful not to spend time dwelling on the enemy. Understanding who he is and how he operates in our lives, where our personal strongholds are and how to be free is sufficient. Everything under the sun offers the opportunity to move beyond health and balance to excesses. It is true here as well. Demons are everywhere but I choose my focus, my gaze to rest on my Lord, Jesus Christ who has defeated him.

There are no formulas for our walk, no discernable paths. My journey will not be yours. My breaking events and spiritual walk will be mine. We share the same truth, the same Jesus Christ and God Almighty but there is a DNA fitted path for each of us to travel. God is imaginative and creative, and He is that way with each of us.

Chapter Five

Love of God

"that He would grant you according to the riches of His glory, to be strengthened with might through His Spirit in the *inner man*, that *Christ* may *dwell in your hearts* through *faith*, that you being rooted and grounded in *love*, may be able to *comprehend* with all the saints what is the *width & length & depth & height- to know the love of Christ* which passes knowledge, *that* you may *be filled with ALL THE FULLNESS OF GOD."!!!!!!* Ephesians 3:16-19.

Knowing God and the depth of His love for me is so important. God Almighty, the Awesome God of the Universe, The God Who created all things LOVES YOU! Yes YOU! Y-O-U!! You. Think about it. Let it go deep into your soul. Ponder this. Spend time gaining a deeper understanding of this fact that God loves you, so that 'you may be filled with all the fullness of God'.

I grew up with some deep self-esteem issues. I grew up believing I was worthless, had little value and not important. The world seemed determined to convince me of the truth of this belief. I was not popular, particularly smart or gifted, not athletic nor graceful. I am, however, what some might think of as a fortunate female. I have blue-eyes and blonde hair with a slender shape. However, when I looked in the mirror, what I saw was my unworthiness staring back at me. My appearance was what

I believed about me. There was no other truth. I believed the absolute worst of me in every way. I believed I was filled with every sort of debauchery and ugliness and deserved nothing. It was devastating to my life. I did not want to go out of my home and would convince my sisters to go shopping with me because I felt unsure of myself. Everything literally filled me with some degree of fear. Things terrified me. Those were usually situations where the truth of me might become known; some event where I would have to speak or do something public, where people would be focused on me. I believed that I would then see mirrored back this confirmation of my worthlessness. People can be cruel intentionally or unintentionally. If I could have hidden throughout life, I thought that would make me happy. I wanted to be left alone and unnoticed.

We can tell when we look at people how they feel about themselves. Poor self-esteem is painful and influences every aspect of your life. It affects the jobs you apply for, the friendships and relationships you attract and keep, the challenges you face. Everything we weigh with the measure of our worthiness. It is our status on the totem pole of life, in the hierarchy of people importance. We fit in to some place in society. This is also self-love. We love ourselves and want others to love us but if we believe we are not special, important it can make us silent, shy, withdrawn and even angry. We withdraw ourselves to protect us from the pain of life. We erect walls and barriers to keep us safe from hurtful relationships. We give and receive based on how we see ourselves. These are layers that cover us.

When God started to refine me, one of the first places I desperately needed His hand was in my self-image. Over time God started to replace my image of me, which began with an honest appraisal of myself. As I started to face myself and my sin, I became convicted and sorrowful which led me to repent of the areas that did not reflect Him. When God started to restore my self-image, He did not make me feel pretty or intelligent; He made me feel special. I was special. He showed me that He had made me for a purpose. He had made me in love and had plans for ME. Realizing that I did not have to BE anything by the world's standards because I no longer needed to measure myself by that criteria gave me freedom to explore who I was created to be; to find my plan and purpose. My identity. I was freed from a wrong personal belief.

Although we will never completely fathom how much or why God loves us, we should spend time trying to **comprehend** it. *God gave us His Son, Jesus Christ, to redeem you and me. We are **that** special! And the love of Christ is evidenced by the Cross. It is a deep truth, a transforming truth.*

God's love for us has nothing to do with our abilities or appearance or intellect. God did not make a mistake when He made you or me! Our appearance, intellect, gifts He INTENDED. And He has plans for us! "Plans for good and not evil, for hope and a future"! He will bring us back from the captivity and bondages of our lives. God made you *'SPECIAL'*. You are no accident. Your appearance is no accident. Your intellect is no accident. Your gifts and talents are no accident. You ARE special; 'Fearfully and wonderfully made' by God FOR God. Our birth is a gift to this world.

We try to make God fit into our limited, finite understanding of ourselves and the world but God calls us out. He wants us to enlarge our perspective, broaden our knowledge and deepen our understanding. He wants us to 'get' Him, know Him, contemplate Him and His love for us and for us to walk daily in the assuredness, in the certainty of that knowledge.

It is personal!

You are special, made deliberately by God to be who you are. You are loved!

You excite God! Every day He is waiting and watching for you to talk to Him, to be aware of His presence in your day. In the same way you awaken excited when in love, remembering that the one you love is alive on this planet, living under the same broad sky, your heart fills with joy and love, excited at the prospect of hearing and seeing your beloved. God is that way with us! I believe that every day He is hoping that I will talk to Him, tell Him I love Him and send thoughts of love and praise His way. I believe we can make God happy and joyful about us. That He can delight in us, personally! He is a personal God and wants a personal, one on one relationship with us. I do not understand how God can love me or want to bother about insignificant me, but He does, passionately, devotedly, completely. He is constant. He never changes. And He loves me. He loves you. We are loved. Get it?

When I seek God, spend time learning who He is, I come to trust Him and He moves heaven on my behalf. He listens.

Love is foundational and the nature of God is love. He is the author of love. Love is very important to God and crucial to us. How or if we are loved will make or break us. Let Him love you. Open your heart and ask Him to fill it with Him. He delights to do this, and He is waiting for you to ask. Seek Him at this moment. Let the realization that you are loved by your Father seep into your soul and let His tender gaze hold your face and His loving smile and delight in you be experienced by you at this moment. Let His sweetness surround you and warm your heart. Embrace Him with your whole heart, accept and return His love. He will not disappoint you.

When God's fullness fills your heart, it will transform your inner landscape. You will not be able to contain His love. It must flow out of you and touch your world.

How would the world look if Christians lived this scripture, lived in the light of this truth? It would change our planet. We would no longer live for ourselves but would live only to please our Father and do His will. And it is our Father's will that His love flow out of us to touch and transform others, reaching them with His love. To esteem others higher than ourselves because we know the truth of ourselves and now understand the gift of God's love, His grace and mercy extended to us, so that we can pass this on. It no longer becomes *about* us. Our lives take on a higher purpose. It will sweeten us and it is His will that His grace and mercy flow from us to others.

Every emotion felt in our heart comes from God. He is interesting, humorous, laughs and cries. He is romantic and tender, gentle and good, kind and caring. He feels sadness and anger. Emotion is a gift and sets us apart from creation. It is a reflection of Him. Remember, we were created in His image. He is fierce and passionate, full of electrical energy and brilliant light, majestic and possessing power unimaginable. He is not complacent and disinterested. His love is active. A relationship with God Almighty is alive, and vibrant.

What I think is crazy is that we are beautiful to Him and His heart is generous towards us and only desires our best. I remind myself when confronted with difficulties with others, that He loves them and they are beautiful to Him and I ask Him to help me to see others as He sees them, to help me walk in love. His love. They are precious souls to Him. Often this changes my relationship with them and changes the situation.

If we could fly at the height of angels and were able to look down upon Earth, we would have a different perspective on the love of God and how much we are loved. If we flew through this universe and surveyed the planets and satellites from Pluto to the Sun we would notice that these planets sit in silent blackness, colorless and dull in their variety of browns and grays, with austere terrains pocked with gullies and craters. We would pass over them unmoved by their mass and un-stimulated by their emptiness. Dust and mist. Dull and seemingly lifeless. And as we pass along from planet to planet we fly above the Earth and hover. There sits a planet with definition and color and so our interest draws us closer. We see oceans and mountains, deserts and forests populated by a vast array of living forms. There are reds, oranges, purples, blues, greens and yellows. It is a planet that is alive and filled with movement. We notice weather, clouds and rainbows. Then we notice a creature so resembling God, whom the angels worship day and night, that we are held in wonder at this creature; at Man. So much interest and detail in this creature and this planet, beauty and variety everywhere. Like nothing observed on the other planets. God's love looks like this planet. Everything the creature needs is available; food, clothing, comforts and relationships to meet emotional, mental and physical needs. All is provided. Love made this planet, love populated it, and love keeps it. The creature is even allowed to curse its creator, rebel and ignore Him and yet His love does not dimmer or fade nor is turned aside by man's contempt, conduct or indifference. He waits for them to love Him. He is constant.

God is romantic. Read Song of Solomon. We are the Bride of Christ and will be in a marriage relationship in Heaven. Love is everything to God. It is the answer. It is the point.

Henri Nouwen wrote in "Finding My Way Home" about a severely handicapped young man named Adam. Mr. Nouwen had gone to live in a residential treatment home for the disabled, as a caregiver. He became the caregiver of a young 25yr old man named Adam. He said that others might describe Adam as "deeply handicapped, an embarrassment, or a burden to caregivers". He had severe epilepsy. Adam could "do nothing for himself, could not speak, cry, laugh and only occasionally made eye contact." But, in being his caregiver, Adam had started to "become his dearest companion." As a result of his taking care of him a love, tenderness and affection started to grow. "Out of what I initially saw as his broken body and broken mind a most beautiful human being emerged, offering me a much greater gift than I would ever be able to offer him." ".. somehow Adam very slowly revealed to me who he was and who I was and how we could love each other." Most of us would write Adam off as useless. Yet he had a purpose in his broken body and he taught others love. He had value. He was special. None of us are an accident or a mistake.

Remember that you are a gift to this world, created by love for a purpose to fulfill. You did not accidentally 'get by' God and arrive here. God is sovereign and in control. God is in His temple. He loves you with passion and devotion, completely. He wants you to comprehend and know His love and to walk in the knowledge that you are loved.

In the words of Oswald Chambers "Your beliefs must become personal possessions."

Believe God loves you! Know God loves you!

Chapter Six

Jesus Christ

As with Satan, I thought I would start this chapter with scriptures introducing the Son of God.

"In the beginning was the Word (Jesus), and the Word was with God, and the Word was God. He was in the beginning with God. All things were made through Him, and without Him nothing was made that was made. In Him was life, and the life was the light of men. And the light shines in the darkness, and the darkness did not comprehend it." John 1:1-5.

"He was in the world, and the world was made through Him, and the world did not know Him. He came to His own (Israel), and His own did not receive Him. But as many as received Him, to them He gave the right to become children of God, to those who believe in His name: who were born, not of blood, nor of the will of the flesh, nor of the will of man, but of God." John 1:10-13.

"And the Word became flesh and dwelt among us, and we beheld His glory, the glory as of the only begotten of the Father, full of grace and truth."

John 1:14.

"He is the image of the invisible God, the firstborn over all creation. For by Him all things were created that are in heaven and that are on earth, visible and invisible, whether thrones or dominions or principalities or powers. All things were created through Him and for Him. And He is before all things, and in Him all things consist. And He is the head of the body, the church, who is the beginning, the firstborn from the dead, that in all things He may have preeminence." Colossians 1:15-18.

Jesus Christ is the Word. He has been since the beginning... With God. He came here with a purpose, to redeem humanity. He came because love sent Him.

Jesus Christ is God. Think about it! God walked among us, put on flesh and entered our world.

I believe it is crucial to understand the cross. When we contemplate God we should pray to have our understanding of Calvary deepened. It is imperative to understand the love God has for us that cost Him so much; His Son and our Lord and Savior Jesus Christ, Who in all His heavenly glory put on humanity. He became fully human and still fully God. He felt everything we feel. Everything that assails us and tempts our minds, emotions and body's assailed and tempted Jesus Christ. Yet the Word says that He did not sin.

It blows me away to think of those two Jewish teenagers, their courage and faith against all odds. The Son of God entering a virgin womb and being born, being nurtured by Mary, having parents, being a child and walking beside His parents holding their hands, sitting on their laps, giving hugs and kisses, smiling, laughing, brushing His teeth and saying His prayers, doing household chores and having brothers and sisters. He went to school and learned a trade. He grew up, went through puberty and became a man. There was a tenor to His voice, a sound peculiar to Him, a walk and a smile that His alone. He hungered and was thirsty. Did He have friends that He confided in? What did He talk to His parents about? What was His relationship with His siblings like? He was God. He walked the planet He created. He wore clothes and had a shoe size. Did girls have a crush on Him? He breathed our air, took in the sights and sounds of this world. He basked in its warmth and shivered in its cold. It rained, the Seasons came and went, and the sun warmed His skin. He experienced it all. He had a life here and this was His generation.

On the night of His birth Bethlehem was surrounded by the vast host of heaven; those majestic and mighty angelic and heavenly beings that surround the throne of God. The sky had been lit with a spectacular star created solely to announce His birth. There was a heavenly choir. Were the remaining heavenly inhabitants hushed, expectant, watching and hovering, tense with wings fluttering and breathless with anticipation? Did they come near to see His birth, God a newborn? Jesus took with Him His Godhead into the confines of a baby boy. Yet Earth was totally unaware of the great and holy event being visited upon it. Mysterious and miraculous.

He was a maverick and confrontational troublemaker. He was and is the **Lion of Judah and the Lamb of God**. You do not have a full image of Him, I believe, if you see Him only as the tender Savior. As the lion, He calmed storms, had mastery over the weather and authority over legions of demons (there was no question of their not obeying Him). He commands all of heaven. Illness, physical imperfections, defects and death were subject to Him. Yet as a lamb, He loved the lost, wretched of life, the poorest of the poor. He hung out with robbers, thieves, prostitutes, every fringe of society, bringing upon Himself the venomous criticism from the religious leaders. But reading the stories of the wretches that He sought and hung with, the adulterous Mary anointing Him with her oil, washing his feet with her tears and drying them with her hair, His exchange with the Samaritan woman at the well, the Roman centurion, His emotion shown in His friendship with Lazarus where Jesus cried, His last chance appeal to Judas, the woman with the issue of blood, tax-collectors, His miraculous feeding of thousands from a few loaves of bread and a couple of fish to His tender embrace of children and their sitting on His lap. All are illustrations of what love looks like and how its liberal, unconditional application changes lives. As a lamb He showed us how to love equally and unbiased. As a lamb, He humbly allowed His arrest, beating and execution. He is coming back as the undefeated warrior King, champion, riding a horse and brandishing a sword, King Jesus.

He was not attractive so as not to ensnare the female heart but He possibly was the closest any individual during that time came to achieving rock star status. I suspect that He was plain in appearance but I also suspect that He was powerful in presence, with His holiness and love pouring out and changing **everything.** Everywhere He went He was followed by masses of people and not for an hour or so on a Wednesday night service, but they left their homes and jobs, took their families and followed Him for days, hungry for His words and His presence. When He entered Jerusalem they lined the streets, laid their clothes and palms on the road as He road by, crying "Hosanna to the Son of David! Blessed is He who comes in the name of the Lord! Hosanna in the highest!" Matthew 21:9.

Jesus had entered into His ministry at the age of thirty. From that time He started the path to Calvary fully aware of the price. It was why He came. As noted with Elisha in 2 Kings 6:17 "And Elisha prayed, and said, 'Lord I pray, open his eyes that he may see.' Then the Lord opened the eyes of the young man, and he saw. And behold, the mountain was full of horses and chariots of fire all around Elisha." How much more than Elisha could Jesus, the Son of God, have summoned the Host of Heaven to come to His aide and defense at any moment? Angels ministered to Him in the wilderness; were Angels amazed watching Jesus, the Son of Almighty God walking amongst humanity? Was this a puzzlement to them? Did they know He was here to redeem humanity by death on the cross?

All the while Satan watched, tempted and waited. If he'd only known.

Jesus gathered to Himself a small group of men whose futures He knew. Their stories were intimately connected to His. He knew their weaknesses, their strengths and their ends. His flesh was having flesh relationships. Is that different then in heaven? They walked, talked, listened, argued, ate and slept near Him. He taught and they listened and learned. All the while the God of Heaven was infiltrating their hearts, igniting their minds and changing their lives. He took humble fishermen and set them on a path that would use these few men to change the world forever.

The below scriptures describe Jesus most powerfully:

Isaiah 53:2 " For He shall grow up before Him as a tender plant, And as a root out of dry ground. He has no form or comeliness; And when we see Him, There is no beauty that we should desire Him.

3 He is despised and rejected by men, a Man of sorrows and acquainted with grief. And we hid, as it were, *our* faces from Him; He was despised, and we did not esteem Him.

4 Surely He has borne our grief's and carried our sorrows; Yet we esteemed Him stricken, smitten by God, and afflicted.

5 But He *was* wounded for our transgressions, He *was* bruised for our iniquities; The Chastisement for our peace *was* upon Him, and by His stripes we are healed.

6 All we like sheep have gone astray; We have turned, everyone to his own way; And the Lord has laid on Him the iniquity of us all.

7 He was oppressed and He was afflicted, Yet He opened not His mouth; He was led as a lamb to the slaughter, and as a sheep before its shearers is silent, So He opened not His mouth.

8 He was taken from prison and from judgment, And who will declare His generation? For He was cut off from the land of the living; For the transgressions of My people He was stricken.

9 And they made His grave with the wicked- but with the rich at His death, because He had done no violence, nor was any deceit found in His mouth.

10 Yet it pleased the Lord to bruise Him; He has put Him to grief, When you make His soul an offering for sin, He shall see *His* seed, He shall prolong *His* days, and the pleasure of the Lord shall proper in His hand.

11 He shall see the labor of His soul, *and* be satisfied. By His knowledge My righteous Servant shall justify many, For He shall bear their iniquities.

12 Therefore I will divide Him a portion with the great, And He shall divide the spoil with the strong, Because

He poured out His soul unto death, And He was numbered with the transgressors, And He bore the sin of many, And made intercession for the transgressors."

Isaiah 52:14 "Just as many were astonished at you, So His visage was marred more than any man, And His form more than the sons of men."

(I believe this scripture is telling us that no one, not one person has been physically defaced *more* than what was inflicted on the human form of our Savior!)

Psalm 22:6 "But I am a worm, and no man; A reproach of men, and despised by the people.

7 All those who see Me ridicule Me; they shoot out their lip, they shake the head, saying

8 He trusted in the Lord, let Him rescue Him; let Him deliver Him, since He delights in Him!

9 But You *are* He who took Me out of the womb; You made Me trust *while* on My mother's breasts.

10 I was cast upon You from birth. From My mother's womb You *have been* My God.

11 Be not far from me, For trouble is near; for *there* is none to help.

12 Many bulls have surrounded Me; strong bulls of Bashan have encircled Me.

13 They gape at Me with their mouths, like a raging and roaring lion.

14 I am poured out like water, and all My bones are out of joint; My heart is like wax; It has melted within Me.

15 My strength is dried up like a potsherd, and My tongue clings to My jaws; You have brought Me to the dust of death.

16 For dogs have surrounded Me; the congregation of the wicked has enclosed Me. They Pierced my hands and feet;

17 I can count all My bones. They look up and stare at Me.

18 They divide My garments among them, and for My clothing they cast lots.

19 But You, O Lord, do not be far from Me; O My strength, hasten to help Me!"

"The Spirit of the Lord God *is* upon Me, because the Lord has anointed Me to preach good tidings to the poor; He has sent Me to heal the brokenhearted, to proclaim liberty to the captives, and the opening of the prison to those who are bound; to proclaim the acceptable year of the Lord." Isaiah 61: 1-2.

I have not personally found any literary work that is more powerful than the narratives found in the Bible. Not only is Scripture powerful, it is alive. Note that these scriptures foretold Christ and His death centuries before His birth. You can recognize the events of the Passion in the above scriptures and they preserve, *before* His death, the enormity of His suffering and His cost!

We can add nothing nor detract anything from the simple and powerful message of the Cross. He came to redeem us because He loved us. Spend time in the Gospels and read the account of His suffering in Gethsemane. In His anguish He sweat blood. He knew what He faced and the suffering that was just ahead but He had made a choice to come and He made a choice to die.

Jesus Christ, He came, He loved, He suffered, He died and now He *LIVES!*

An important fact about Calvary is that all sin, its vast filth, every depravity and evil, every by-product of Satan entered the flesh of Jesus; it became part of Him. The full depth of sin in all its horror and depraved twisted sickness and darkness Christ experienced. Chesterton points out that Christ had in His flesh all the elements of being an atheist, a murderer, a molester, a thief, on and on... He <u>bore</u> our sins. Literally. It is more heinous because He was *innocent* and yet He remained the pure Lamb of God.

We cannot say to God "You don't understand, You don't know my troubles or the depth of my pain!" Because of what Christ experienced on the Cross, He is now able to be fully our intercessor and there is *nothing* that we can experience that Christ did not personally *know* at that time spent on the Cross. It is why He is affective as our mediator and intercessor before God. He can explain us, He understands us and He KNOWS our suffering.

BLOOD SACRIFICE

Life and sin are in the blood. The blood is a crucial element in the salvation process. In the Old Testament, before Calvary, Israel removed their personal sin by laying their hands on a spotless lamb and through the sacrifice of the lamb and shedding its blood, their sin was transferred and thereby removed. And so it is with our precious Savior. He is our Spotless Lamb, the Lamb of Cod. His death on the Cross transferred our sin unto Him and He fully paid the penalty for our sins, for every person who accepts Jesus Christ. The heredity of sin obtained in the Garden of Eden was broken at Calvary. It was a transfer of sin from our blood to Christ's.

In the movie, 'Narnia', based on a book by C.S. Lewis, Jesus is represented by the lion, Aslan. As was pointed out in the story, with the betrayal by Edward, the laws in Narnia demanded justice for his crime, which was death. The law had to be obeyed and judgment satisfied; not taking the life of Edward would violate the law and unravel Narnia. The law was foundational. There could be no favorites, exceptions. Justice must be blind to persons. But unforeseen by the witch (and Satan), there could be a *substitute*! Adam betrayed God in the Garden and the justice of God demanded the consequence of death and separation from God. God could not play favorites with Adam (and mankind) and remain a just and holy God and *so Jesus Christ came to be our substitute*, to satisfy the law, to redeem us and gain us heaven and communion with God, our Father. We are now able to enter into the presence of God because of the Cross!

G.K. Chesterton in "Orthodoxy" had some interesting revelations about Calvary for me. He reminds us that our Godhead is a Society, the Trinity. The Father, The Son and The Holy Spirit. God has always been relational; about fellowship; separate yet One. Chesterton also points out that the Trinity was *separated* on the Cross! At the moment of Christ's death God Almighty and His Son, Jesus Christ, were torn from each other just as the curtain separating the Holy of Holies was torn in the temple. In that moment, because Jesus had taken upon Himself our sin and because of the holiness of God and the fact that sin could not survive in His presence God, the Father had to separate Himself, turn His head away from His Son. I suspect that nothing Christ suffered up until then was as great as the suffering this separation caused Him. He was no longer apart of God His Father! He was totally alone. When in Time had this ever happened before?

Psalm 22 starts out with this moving narrative "My God, My God, why have You forsaken Me? Why are You so far from helping Me, and from the words of my groaning?"

Mark 15:34 reports the same comment" My God, My God, why have You forsaken Me?"

When I consider those breaking moments in my life against the cost of the Cross, the suffering of my Savior, I am moved to humility. They pale in comparison and seem little to ask of me, especially when the results of them bring so much grace and mercy from God. His favor shining on me!

"I am the bread of life. Your fathers ate the manna in the wilderness and are dead. This is the bread which comes down from heaven, that one may eat of it and not die. I am the living bread which came down from heaven. If anyone eats of this bread, he will live forever; and the bread that I shall give is My flesh, which I shall give for the life of the world." John 6:48-51.

"Most assuredly, I say to you, unless you eat the flesh of the Son of Man and drink His blood, you have no life in you. Whoever eats My flesh and drinks My blood has eternal life, and I will raise him up at the last day. For My flesh is food indeed, and My blood is drink indeed. He who eats My flesh and drinks My blood abides in Me, and I in him." John 6:53-57. "He who eats this bread will live forever." John 6:58.

He is broken bread and poured out wine. This is a powerful sacrament that we observe in our churches where we honor Him and remember His sacrifice by participating in sharing His flesh and blood. We share in His cost, His suffering and His love. It is a continual reminder of His broken body and shed blood. I am *in Him* and He is *in me*.

It is comfortable for us to accept the concept of a non-defined and vague god; some god, even God Himself. But why do so many stumble over Jesus Christ? I believe we stumble over Jesus and run from acknowledging Him because to acknowledge Him we have to recognize something about ourselves. We acknowledge our weakness and the fact that we are sinners. We experience a breaking event by the acknowledgment of our need for Him. We have to face the Cross. We can keep our false identity and pride with 'a' god but *Jesus Christ makes it personal!* This acknowledgment goes straight to our hearts and we are forever changed.

FORGIVENESS / LOVE ARE DECISIONS

We are commanded to love and to forgive. Most of us believe that these are emotions but they are choices, decisions. The emotions follow, usually. We must choose to love and we must choose to forgive. When we understand the Cross, that the full filth of humanity visited the flesh of our Lord and yet He said 'Father forgive them' we come to understand the imperative in the command that His forgiveness was not based on any *merit* of the 'them' and nothing we experience is darker, more severe than what Christ experienced on the Cross. We are left without excuse when we choose not to forgive.

If we actually think this through, how can we tell God we will not forgive? We may believe that the pain *we* experienced is too deep, the harm done too horrible and to forgive is to release the person or situation from paying some consequence. There is a need deep in us that cries out for justice, retribution. But when we wash that through the cost of the Cross it losses its power to persuade. There is a parable in the Bible where Jesus tells a story about this servant who owed his King 'ten thousand talents'. The servant begged for mercy from the King and he found it. The King forgave this enormous debt that the servant could not have repaid. The servant then left the King and, in the street, sees another servant that owed him 'a hundred denarii'. The first servant ignores the pleas for mercy from the other servant and has the man thrown into debtor's prison. The King learns of this action and calls this first servant before him. The King says "You wicked servant! I forgave you all that debt because you begged me. Should you not also have had compassion on your fellow servant, just as I had pity on you? And his master (the King) was angry, and delivered him to the torturers until he should pay all that was due to him." Matthew 18:23-34

We are commanded to forgive because we are forgiven. **Forgiveness releases us from the power of the pain and memory and heals us**. God knows what is good for us and He knows that this will restore us and set us free from the situation. If we do not forgive, like the first servant, our refusal to forgive torments and tortures our life. We remain a victim and a slave to the memory and the pain. When we obey God, even when we feel devastating pain, *by forgiving the other person it releases the power of the event over us and helps us move past it into liberty and freedom.* We can leave the matter in God's hands to judge and punish. God is just and fair and loves the other person as much as He loves us, but He will also chastise and correct the person that harmed us in a way that will deeply reach that person. We can trust our Father to handle this matter and leave it. It releases us and brings blessings into our lives.

The same is true of love. We are commanded to love. There are many less than loveable people that we encounter in our lives. They present a challenge to our walking in the obedience of this command. I have to ask God to help me see the person the way He sees the person. God loves them. And so must I. I step out in an act of love and find that joy springs up in my heart from being obedient. Love for that person often follows! God *is* good and He *is* grace and mercy. We must be about our Father's business.

I hear often that believing only in Jesus Christ is narrow-minded. It is. It is also certain that if there was another way, and most religions today predate the Cross and yet could not save us, God would not have asked the Son of His love, to enter humanity, suffer and die. Therefore, the answer to our redemption came in the form of our Savior. It is also certain that God will not allow any argument or defense to gain us entrance to Heaven that circumvents the Cross. To do so would be for God to negate the cost of the Cross and those 12 hours, to make Christ's coming, suffering and dying, pointless. If we could have gotten there any other way, then the Cross was unnecessary.

Keeping our focus on the Cross helps us to be humble, to love and forgive and to esteem others higher than ourselves. We should *often* spend time contemplating the Passion, those twelve hours and the life of Christ. There is power in this. It will keep us humble remembering His cost and our sin and the greatness of His love for us!

As Simon Peter says in John 6: 68-69 to Jesus when Jesus asked if the twelve disciples would also desert Him, Peter said,

"Lord, to whom shall we go? You have the words of eternal life. Also we have come to believe and know that You are the Christ, the Son of the living God." To whom can we turn except to Him Who has power to save our souls. He is the Son of the living God.

"For I determined not to know anything among you, except Jesus Christ and Him crucified." 1Cor 2:2.

"And lo, I am with you always, even to the end of the age." Matthew 28:20

"In the world you will have tribulation; but be of good cheer, I have overcome the world." John 16:33b

---

Chapter Seven

Salvation

Throughout our lives God woos and calls us to Him. At each of these moments, and some of us have many, we weigh the call of God against our lives. His quiet voice speaks to our hearts and asks us to look to Him. At these moments we know we are being confronted with a spiritual decision. We look at our lives and filter the moment through the cost of rebirth, the cost of choosing God. We examine things we believe we may need to give up, turn from or abandon. We consider the cost and make a decision.

I pray that is book helps you say yes to God calling you, Yes to our Lord and Savior, Jesus Christ.

"For God so loved the world that He gave His only begotten Son, that whoever believes in Him should not perish but have everlasting life" John 3:16

If you are ready, pray with me, "Father God, Lord God Almighty, I acknowledged that Jesus Christ lived, died and rose again for my salvation. I confess my sins and ask Jesus into my heart. Amen"

Heaven Awaits!!!!

About the Author

Kari DuMouchel Parker is a voice of hope for those navigating the complexities of faith in today's times. Following a transformative spiritual renewal in 2006, Kari dedicated her life to studying the Word and understanding the heart of the Creator. Her writing is shaped by a mother's resilience and a profound personal history of overcoming life's most crushing trials—including her son's survival of spinal meningitis—through abandoned confidence in God.